We Grow Tomatoes in Tiny Towns

We Grow Tomatoes in Tiny Towns

by Jeremy Jusek

We Grow Tomatoes in Tiny Towns
Copyright © 2019 by Jeremy Jusek.

All Rights Reserved
Published by Unsolicited Press
Printed in the United States of America.

All rights reserved. Printed in the United States of America. No part of this book may be used or reproduced in any manner whatsoever without written permission except in the case of brief quotations embodied in critical articles or reviews.

Attention schools and businesses: for discounted copies on large orders, please contact the publisher directly.

For information contact:
Unsolicited Press
Portland, Oregon
www.unsolicitedpress.com
orders@unsolicitedpress.com
619-354-8005

Book and Cover design by Editor:

ISBN: 978-1-947021-74-7

10 9 8 7 6 5 4 3 2 1

Contents

Sailing the Atlantic Without a Compass	13
The Garrettsville Boardwalk	14
Emma: A Poem	15
4 AM	17
Brad's Liquor Stop	18
State Route 422	19
Withering	20
Newspaper Morning	21
The Guardians of Bancroft	22
Parking Lot Paint	24
Lotto Ticket	25
Cigarettes	27
Emma's Voice	28
I Wish I'd Taken More Pictures	29
Elmer's Gift	30
White Haven	33
Cobwebs	34
Portage County Fair	38
Living Walls	40
Nelson Ledges State Park	41
A Surrealist's Practical Advice to Spoons	42
We Grow Tomatoes in Tiny Towns	44
Breakfast	47
Fluid Motion	48
Finding My Center in Giant Eagle on a Tuesday Morning	49
Colleen Drinks to Think	51
5k in Ravenna	52
The Pastor's Gift	54
Emma Performs My Baptism	55
Gravel Laid Under Concrete	56
The Body	57

Family Practice	58
Headwaters Trail	59
The Floral-Patterned Couch	61
What it Means to Shed Skin	62
Richard's Remains	63
Running Wild	64
Interstate 77 in '07	66
The White Birch Grove	67
Twelve Years Later I Return Home	68
The Recurring Dream	70
The Surgeon That Operates in the Dark	72
The Hero Hunt	73
What I Pursue on Walks	74
Emma, Whom I Met in Death	76
Acknowledgments	79
About the Author	81
About the Press	82

Introduction

The man's hand pulls the woman's eyelids apart. He slices her eye with a razor, which briefly becomes a thin cloud slicing the moon, before gel oozes out of the cut eyeball. During this well-known scene from Salvador Dali and Luis Buñel's surrealist film, *Un Chien Andalou*, I looked over at my students' faces. We were in a classroom at the University of Edinburgh and though the room was dark (no doubt due to Scotland's constant cloudy weather), I was able to make out the faces of the poets in the room. One, Jeremy Jusek, seemed especially rapt.

By that time, I had been reading Jusek's work for a year. In fact, his poems inspired my choice to show *Un Chien Andalou* that day. When it comes to the dreamlike moments in *We Grow Tomatoes in Tiny Towns*, this strangeness has a name, Emma, and her recurring character is the very incarnation of surrealism, a movement known for its use of the unconscious mind to push creativity in art. Most might imagine Dali's melting clocks in *The Persistence of Memory*, but here (specifically in "Emma Performs My Baptism"), Jusek gives us his version of morphing images: "Emma is a firecracker and bursts into flames. / I dipped my hand into a well, but I've / only found marrow." She often appears as a kind of shadow to the speaker or an imaginary friend, taking him and us into the surreal almost as a resistance to any kind of stagnation.

She first appears in "Emma: A Poem," as a possible solution to the problem of disorder:

Emma wipes beetles from the marred windowpanes, throws
open the glass to let the outside breeze in, and greets
great, violet drops of rain.

Now every color is glittering oil,
swelling organic mass. The world is slick
with beetle shells. My world
is finally in order.

In this same poem, there are references to Jane and Frank, an allusion to Jane Austen's *Emma*, but this version of Emma can be better imagined as "a tattooed princess licking thorns," as she is described in the poem "Emma's Voice." Like Austen's character, Jusek's Emma is attempting to help others, but her attempts prove to be destructive, showing us that she is ultimately responsible for disorder. Here, it's like she's a part of the speaker's unstable mind, even performing surgery on the speaker in "The Surgeon That Operates in the Dark." After she makes an incision with a "rusted / scalpel in her unwashed hands," the speaker describes her work: "Her blouse / is stuffed into my open / chest cavity, reckless love," and

She stitches me up with
the care of a rabid beaver
gnawing logs, damming
my smoky tumors inside
with the blood-soaked blouse.

Emma's violence resists the speaker's everyday mundane, resists the small town in Ohio where he appears to be stuck, much like the cicadas that can't reach the surface in Jusek's poem "State Route 422": "Cicadas crest their call. Flitting. /

Chittering. Some couldn't surface, // they're stuck after seventeen years, / under fresh concrete." He is caught in the midst of many comparisons, boyhood and manhood, real and surreal, but mostly the speaker is pulled between decay and new growth. There are splinters, peeling paint, burning trash, a stuffed bear with a "ripped ear," and even Mother Nature smokes a cigar, yet tomatoes are cultivated and babies are born and "crying / in baby powder like kneaded bread." Often, the new growth stems directly from decay, as is the case in the title poem, "We Grow Tomatoes in Tiny Towns." When a corpse, Greg, decomposes into the nearby creek that waters the townspeople's tomatoes, there are "bits of Greg / glowing in their fruit."

Emma is not the only character worth noting here. In fact, she is always juxtaposed against the realism of characters and their movements within Garrettsville and Bancroft. Pastor John, one of many characters struggling with alcoholism and addiction, still manages to project a reasonable voice and is as almost godfatherly to the speaker, gifting him a mysterious bunny-shaped key. (I'll note here that the white rabbits in this collection are not from Wonderland, but a darker reality; the speaker does not chase after them and in "The Floral-Patterned Couch," their ears inexplicably bleed.) This struggle is shared with others in the book, such as Colleen, someone everyone in the town knows, and Ethan, a young man struggling with drugs. Another of the town's curious characters includes the appropriately named Elmer, a farmer, who doesn't mind sharing a beer with both Pastor John and the speaker, and many others that color the place of which the speaker finally claims (with another reference to Jane Austen's work):

To come full-circle out of Garrettsville
I buried my various prejudices, combated
pride. I'll take the town with me wherever I go
as long as I'm still alive.

Although echoes of John Berryman's *Dream Songs* and the work of John Ashbery exist, Jusek's poems are truly his own, identifiable by their dank strangeness. His poetry often moves beyond what our eyes expect to see, zig-zagging between the real and the surreal. Dali once said, "Surrealism is destructive, but it destroys only what it considers to be shackles limiting our vision." Amidst poems that present the realism of a small Ohio town, Jusek's work does just that.

Genevieve Betts
Arcadia University
January 2019

For my dearest, Sara.

Sailing the Atlantic Without a Compass

A stained-glass window
emerges above my head,
turning into a mosaic porthole
around which wood spreads.

This usually happens on Saturday,
but sometimes always, too. I know
when it is coming—my hands web, eyes
harden, sea foam sifts through my kidneys.

Like the minute hand on a clock
the boat rides the same waves,
rising up and returning to position.

Without the stars we would anguish,
break chairs on the quarterdeck,
bobbing and breathing and seething.

Foolishness is finding safety
in uncluttered violence.
At night, the toys would return
to the wooden chest

locked until morning, and I'd clutch
a stuffed animal, the bear with
the ripped ear, sailing the waves
into calm anarchy.

The Garrettsville Boardwalk

The wood grain is like fingerprints,
coarse DNA of this rattlesnake town.
I know where to lift my hand

to avoid splinters.
The brick wall behind Subway,
ivy-hugged, propped our shoulders

when I— during my— that middle school
kiss. I remember the sloppy half-moons
of her lips, like punctured tangerines.

Eagle Creek splashes bubbling code.
The finest cryptographers could learn
a thing or two from our pickle farmers.

Under the walk, biology students
carve holes in the ecosystem
with nets and formaldehyde jars.

Minnows dart around their bare
toes. Mine have five hundred feet
to walk with nowhere to go.

Emma: A Poem

Emma sat in empty space
where my couch used to be.
I grabbed a beer from the fridge
and asked if modern Gods
drink. They do.

We drank to every blue profile,
to mountains resting on our feet,
the ridges and valleys were lagers
until the sunset. The sun, a crimson
bottle cap falling from the sky.

Emma was tearing up my floorboards
letting the vines, June beetles and worms in.
The green wrinkled into sludge,
runny tendrils seeping into loose soil.

After we pondered the colors, Emma.
It was never Emma. Even after the termites
crawled up her legs and burrowed
somewhere high.

Yesterday Emma was a bowl of oatmeal,
today she brings her friends Jane and Frank
who watch her make a sweater from the cables and wires
criss-crossing my house.

As Frank prepares charades, Emma said the
knit needed to be closer, and I listened.
When she knelt beside me I sniffed her hair.

I threw out my old shirt, an android weave,
tiny scaffolding made of severed steel. The beetles keep
marching inward, covering the furniture. The love seat
glimmers from their scaly, oil-colored scarab shells.

Emma laughs her joke at Jane, a kind of
grayscale Dixon line. Frank knows
she knows. I don't know anything.
I let the charades speak for themselves.

Emma wipes beetles from the marred windowpanes, throws
open the glass to let the outside breeze in, and greets
great, violet drops of rain.

Now every color is glittering oil,
swelling organic mass. The world is slick
with beetle shells. My world
is finally in order.

4 AM

The oak porch, peeling, creaks
    in tune with my knees.
        Another kind of heartbeat.

The ambassadors of morning,
    dew and mist, vanish.

Brad's Liquor Stop

I've found in my late twenties
I get carded for boxed wine
but not Chardonnay.

The white paint is peeling
outside of the drive-through.
The snow falls.

The countryside sits in
haunting stillness while I silently
stare back, just as it taught me.

A ragged woman stands smoking, eyes shut, leaning against
the building's better side.
It's Colleen and her shark-tooth necklace.

Brad waves to Dan who pulls his F150
around back, popping the gas. Dan falls
asleep, his camo ushanka resting on the wheel.

A small rat crosses rutted tire tracks,
steps over her mother's skeleton
and falls asleep next to a heat vent.

This beautiful country town: weathered by
harsh natural order, and organized by chaos.

State Route 422

Grass tickles the garden spider,
his legs yellow sticks cradling dew.

Cicadas crest their call. Flitting.
Chittering. Some couldn't surface,

they're stuck after seventeen years,
under fresh concrete.

Hay bales rot along the pavement.
The best bundles were stolen

after Elmer died
and his goats starved.

A deer gazes blankly,
clover stuck in its fur.

Cars whiz by the spider
who spins, unconcerned.

Withering

A lonely mother gasps into moldy
bathroom tile. She shivers, trying
to remember Jonathan's name.

He'll miss her peripheral glances,
preference for brightly-colored blown
glass, winding lectures on GMOs and advice

on the best wheat pancake mix recipe,
all of it and more a fallen rain gauge filled
with dirt among last Autumn's leaves.

Sulfur is in the sink's strainer,
wafting past the radiator to mingle
with *Aspergillus* under the tub.

The fentanyl-laced heroin takes hold
and Jonathan is forgotten. Small comfort,
his name—the last thing on her dying lips.

Newspaper Morning

A dead bird hit my window,
thrown by the paper boy.

I chased him down and begged
for, next week, a broken window.

He handed me magic beans
which I sprinkled on the corpse.

I crushed the robin into my porch
with a steel-toed boot. I now can't leave

my house through the front door.
It's that damned beanstalk.

Three weeks later a nest was built
outside my kitchen window. Two.

Twenty. So many
I now crack the eggs into my laundry.

I like to see the yellow embryos mix
into bubbles through my washer's glass hood.

The Guardians of Bancroft

Pastor John talks of ghosts
all the time. His sermons
are bored but paranoid.
My ghost is an imaginary friend
who hides in snow banks,
a mirage mouthing translations
for other spirits in the woods.

Under cracked bark
my feet slip on moss.
Bancroft is snow-slathered.
Birch branches droop under snow
and over slouched bodies.
Naked, but for the rattlesnake
marks, faces polluted with ash.

They lead me to Glasir, its worn
leaves weakly swatting the sun.
Here God is not welcome.
Finches laugh at my youth
like my uncles all do.

Within the stillness, a deer
melts into shadows
behind a legion of branches.

Inside a stump chittering is
an overweight, man-sized squirrel
named Elmer.

My friend tells me Elmer is waiting
for his wife.

How sad—for Mary will surely
haunt her parents' farm in Pittsburgh.

Parking Lot Paint

The car's cubicle—
self-indulgent strips of yellow.
Fescue and clover, battered by tires,
grasp, crushed breathless under rubber.
On the happiest days I wonder
if I'll outlive my parking space.

In between the last two coats
I had seven haircuts. I think too much
about weaponizing mineral spirits.

It would happen on a Sunday.
During the drive over I'd cradle
mineral spirits, the metal can
digging into my ribcage.

The sky would barely throb violet,
a starburst bruise pulsing
where the sun fought to dismiss
my stealth. By the time the sun cleared
the horizon, the acrylic coffin's
slush melt is gone.

The only incriminating evidence
—cigarette butt stains.

Lotto Ticket

Amanda (I went to school with her)
and Richard (A Birmingham chav)
are once again at the counter.

The attendant turns on the fan.
Shavings cluster in wispy mini-vortexes
and tumble across the blue veins
running along Amanda's hands.
tumble across hands protruding veins.
1992 was cruel to Amanda's fingers.

She turns to leave, then fishes a fresh bill.
You can almost hear her eyelids thud shut
as she scans the $20 options. "*Better chance
of winning.*" I think the attendant said it.
He is reading from a tabloid.

When I walk up with my coffee
I smell Amanda. Her breath is like
stale car freshener (Pine).

The bubbly numbers, orange outlining
a unique combination of smiles
envelop cherries and crocodiles.

Richard flips a five, positions his coat
to hide his pant stains, and leaves with whiskey.

Amanda just scribbles. The poster for last
month's fair, free of the tape,
curls around her arm.

I wave myself out.
At the pump I light up,
the cigarette smoke unfurling about my neck.
An erring slipstream pulls it up my nostrils—
a tiny wisp of ghost patting me down.
Every last cigarette is sweetest
surrounded by gasoline.

Cigarettes

My right to fright
is fluid freight
evaporating inside
the hollowed tunnels
of selfish pride.

Emma's Voice

Emma takes me places.
And she warns me that angry
people are not always wise.

We lift into black rain after
the neighbors fall asleep. Her breath
makes the water prismatic.

I've heard tales of women
with hair made of tangled snakes.
Hers is a mattress of daggers.

Driving to and from work
her voice is anesthetic.
She screams with Cleveland's police sirens.

It's the us, the Emma wrapped
together, a man being rescued
by a tattooed princess licking thorns.

I never heard sirens on Bancroft. Emma believes in the
whispers of a loaded pistol. Her will
is curtains fluttering just outside my skull.

I Wish I'd Taken More Pictures

Lasting latex bobs, a craft, one-man, floating
in the ocean. The salesman sold me extra space
for entertainment, so I forgot to bring food.

Or a compass. Or pictures. Like that one photo,
the one of my infant daughter, naked, crying
in baby powder like kneaded bread.

If I drink small amounts, I can survive
on brine. Memories aren't fresh,
and I desperately need a water filter.

Seaweed bobs alongside the raft.
I dip my cracked fingers into the ocean
and lay the green slime along the rubber edge.

My favorite picture is in a black frame.
Although my daughter is crying, wearing
only boots and a diaper,
she had just drawn her first circle.

She was so happy
and I was so happy
because she had built her first raft
using only a crayon and paper.

Elmer's Gift

*Farming looks mighty easy when your
plow is a pencil and you're a thousand
miles from the corn field.*
    - Dwight D Eisenhower

Sharp, bristling stems dug into my shins
as I listened to this kind man, the kind of man

Nature molds with her bare hands
to remind the world of raw gentility given

physical form. Elmer's form is round,
like a weathered stone, wise in life, and

as rich in Earthly manner as the Earth itself.
This was a man who taught me the key

to spotting shallow rabbit nests, how to store
hay, how to stay awake during Sunday sermons,

and why God wouldn't care if I fell asleep.

I tried to leave when he confessed his fears
over beers to Pastor John. "Stay, sit," he said.

"Sometimes you can't sort the wheat from the chaff." That is
when Elmer handed me a beer.

There in this field I learned a man among men,
for farmers a model 10 out of 10, was afraid

of God, of whiskey, of dying in his armchair
alone, of saying goodbye on the phone to his son

without knowing when the last phone call might come. He
feared next year's harvest, losing

corn and soybean subsidies, global warming,
his unleashed dog getting hit on 422.

John nodded, never prodded, sipping along.

What is the consensus on non-abusive drunks?
I wondered this often as ever more men

drowned themselves around me, it's like they found me—or
just maybe that many were lost.

Pastor John, an honest man of God if there
were ever twenty-four hours to a day

in his stumbling, drunken way he put a hand
on Elmer's shoulder and said "Do not rest

until God goes and makes you dead."
The rest that follows long ceased clattering

around in my head. Now both are dead.

But I learned that day the salt of the Earth tastes different
than the kind Morton makes.

That night Elmer, the stoic towering dad
of six children long gone, he gave me his song.

It's masculine to reflect on where we've gone wrong, manly
to bray to keep the demons away.

And after, when we sprayed down the tomatoes,
I knew the salt with which Garrettsville is spiced

would stick with me the rest of my life.

White Haven

Drunk by 10 AM, Pastor John
gathers sticks. Some have lost
their bark, bite marks from Spot.

The grass leans in unfamiliar patterns.
He'd been used to the wavy commentary,
conversation from the prior year.

Like a vacuumed carpet
rushed blades roamed in rows,
surprisingly uniform, chattering,
until John vomits on his audience.

People see this on the regular.
But we all love John and respect
his privacy. So nobody does
        anything.

Cobwebs

I

Spring nudges like a caterpillar,
but summer is the sun's glint
on ants being crushed
in a wolf spider's maw.

I hurl hatchets at a dead tree trunk.
Hundreds of flies die around me,
lifespan spent as the sun sets.
I am fucking angry.

A lantern stutters, a wire noose
pulls light into the porch ceiling,
forever up, up, up.

II

The most epic men are unknown.
Face-down in caves far below the Earth,
chitin grows from their dust.

The mushrooms simply think
explorers are redundant.

I don't chase white rabbits underground.
Pollen now collects on the grill,

a shuffling caterpillar
is leaving a metallic trail.

III

My paperbacks smell like campfire
and cigarette smoke, stinging
tar, curling yellow.

I planted phlox and milkweed
for the butterflies, but
I only ever notice the squirrels.

Time chips wrinkles into our faces,
but words were always the dynamite
that built railroads.

IV

I expect nights by a fire
to wrap like an ember cocoon.
As it turns out, Huckleberry Finn's raft
was just a raft moving on, on, on.

I have dreams about birds
washing my car and deer
driving me to work.
Maybe if I could adjust the wind
my clothes would always be dry.

There are a few carrots still,
dead in the garden.
Premature orange nubs with
faded shoots strangled
by nettle and timothy.

The *shffftipp* of lighting matches
smells the best in the sharp snap
of falling snow. I like
confusing tobacco with cold breath.

V

I stood above the oil spill.
Hands in my jeans I watched
the dirt choke to death.

Once I woke from a dream
while camping to see spider
silhouettes, like thin fingers,
tapping atop the tent. Now
when it rains I timidly look to
earthworms instead of butterflies.

Mother Nature wears straw hats
as summer unrolls like sod.
She groomed me to resurrect
bald eagles and stave venom.

She often pauses to remove her gloves
before taking a cigar drag.
You'd never catch Nature

chewing on wheat.

Portage County Fair

Lucy is five years old today and drunk—
her father is letting her celebrate
with Black Velvet Irish whiskey.

It's non-caffeinated. After all,
caffeine stunts growth.

She clutches a stuffed giraffe
downwind of the lotto dump cows.

Under the bleachers a teenager
gets pregnant. The tractor pull
roars under camera flash applause.

A dehydrated pig collapses, feebly sweating.
Lucy cries. If God wanted empathy
understood, he'd have provided pamphlets.

The pig's owner cries too, because
she spent her summer earnings
on high octane fitter feed.

Feet crush popcorn into dirt.
Charlotte never told Templeton about
the free market rat scrap competition.

Lucy pauses a moment from tugging
her dad's sleeve. He snores on coarse
plywood—the makeshift bar on the north side.

Hundreds of other families stream home,
intact. They know Lucy. Colleen, you know her,
she'll pick up the pieces.

Living Walls

I don't remember when I first registered yelling. My mother's voice had cadence. She would have sounded like a drill sergeant but for the fear. My father sounded like a fridge tipping over and its contents flooding the hollow tile. Those sounds reverberated through the walls.

After dark I would press my ear to the peeling paint and the walls breathed. They heard it all, too. When they informed me we were moving I smashed my Wolfpack Lego castle and ripped apart some stuffed animals in a wave of self-loathing. I dumped the shredded cotton bodies in the corroded horse stables behind our house. Years later I would find a scratched eye and wonder if I could uninvite loneliness.

When my chest felt tight, or the kudzu had again covered my bedroom windows and I became trapped, the walls breathed with me. I could feel the dryness in their bones when the wind whipped through, piercing where insulation should have been. Every violently-burst pipe is a Rastafarian hemorrhage, cozy TLC, a reminder that deer bed in the snow without first checking the weather.

At night I'd sneak out and pretend I was one of the farm horses, galloping down an empty Bancroft. I passed paternal fealty to the man on the moon. He always smiled. And when I returned home the walls would greet me. It was my first glimpse into old age, long before I learned how to apologize.

Nelson Ledges State Park

I can drink the souls of glaciers
and try when I close my eyes.
This is the thrill of giants
hurling boulders. Three-storey
icicles sweat, refracting moss and spiders.

Through gritty monuments of stone
and towering oak trees,
paths wag a finger at Nature,
zooming up, down, over and through
precarious pockets of erosion.

Alan the park ranger
prods slumped bodies draped
in leather and dyed wool with
a walking stick. He chuckles
and drags on a hand-rolled cigarette.

Farmers are out for the Flea Market Auction.
Hands cracked, swollen and cut,
clothes stamped by campfire smoke,
they recline on mossy stones
drunk on homemade lager.

A Surrealist's Practical Advice to Spoons

I told them again and again,
birthdays are fun-house only
if you reflect the skinny side.
Kaleidoscope faces scare me—
images warped in glossy jubilation
like a gas station urinal.

I keep my spoons in the basement.
I tell them fingerprints easily mar
the surface because spoons are Q-tips
for giants, a primitive way to silence
candles, medieval nose-guards.

I spin tales of spoons saving daffodils
from new construction projects
and of Alexander who slayed Copperthor
with an enchanted soup ladle.

Then I show them pictures of parties
and spoons, frilly, white, doused in sugar.
Spoons clanking songs, sneering
at disposables, and playing volleyball
in my courtyard. Spooning oatmeal.
Laying divided in the silverware drawer,
snugly spooning together.

When I ask if they are ready to behave
they bristle like forks and tell me to

go fuck myself.

We Grow Tomatoes in Tiny Towns

I - The City

is a bruise, glowing. Earth's eczema,
a golem forever marching downward.
If a fire cleansed the traffic lights
and coughing smoke stacks, I like to think
we would have left an impression.
A reverse meteor digging a canyon
millions of years faster than flowing water.

Windows blink as cars stream past
illuminating lives around me. I see
a man watching *Law & Order: SVU*,
scratching at the back of his head.
A stippled toddler pastes a kitchen wall
while a dog begs for food. The horizon's
pink has turned purple. We have all this
pollution, but forgot to enjoy sunsets.
We have corpses in dumpsters, because
the Cuyahoga is dredged. How long
has it been since the heights were littered
with trees?

II - The Corpse

Greg was a hated man in May.
After dressing the body
and taking selfies
and distributing CDs
they found under ruined
leather seats in his truck,
they dumped his body
in the snaking creek.
The corpse will take weeks
to decompose. Greg's memories
will decay much faster.

The cracks begin in July.
Single-shoot blossoms bristle
rebellion from the liver.
From a leak in the veins
blood and brine
flow over crickets.
His nutrients will be fed on
by deer lapping at the creek,
by us when the tomato farms
pump their fields, bits of Greg
growing in their fruit.

III - The Produce Stand

Cleveland State students frequently stop
at the organic stand at the edge of 422.
Commuters so easily ignore our
revolving lives and swinging screen doors.

Greg now costs 25 cents apiece, he rests with
a softened pile of swollen heads with little green hats. He
will be mashed into sauce
and forgotten in little, plastic drawers.

A whole bushel of unbought Greg was tossed aside and
rotted with a deer carcass all through August. Elsewhere,
Elmer's electricity was shut off and his haphazard shack
condemned.

Breakfast

A flickering light sheds silently
over Ethan's obscured body.
The next street over
his mother is cooking eggs.

There are nightmares tucked
in the blanket folds. The piles
of dirt and rags and feces
are simply insulation.

Morning chill sweeps in smoke
through a broken window.
Outside Roy is burning trash.

Ethan stirs, his hand running
along chalky holes in drywall.
He senses the day beginning.
Not from the sun, but the
raspy fingers clawing between
his heart and lungs.

Ethan checks for blood
in his needle before slamming.
The bacon finishes just in time
with the coffee and eggs. His mother
calls for her dreaming drugged-out son.

Fluid Motion

I stored some memories in a bottle
when I was nine. I didn't find it again
for twenty years.

My hands crack when I run and shake
when I slice vegetables. The tomatoes,
jealous, demand I cry when I cut them, too.

Pushing thirty years I've learned my hands,
they do terrible things under pressure.
Now the bottle, well, it smells like whiskey.

I am finally mature enough to drink coffee.
When I hug my uncovered body pillow
I'm caught in a waltz with a girl in a pink

chiffon dress and bright, curly
ideas about fire. The song ends
so I pour the pitcher on her head—
but I've simply greased the flames.

Finding My Center in Giant Eagle on a Tuesday Morning

Mary is sampling the olives,
licking her fingers clean.
She just left the bathroom.

Garth Brooks crackles over
the PA system like a transistor radio
catching signal from Route 88.

Colleen (everyone knows Colleen) waddles
to a shelf with all the confidence you'd suspect
after thirty years of social work.

I stand in the center of the store
forgetting why I'm here. I generate
my own gravity, but far less than the moon.

My crisis has expired like the mayo in my hand.
Mary is now arguing with the cashier
about coupons. Macabre costs seventy cents.

The tangerine jars are dusty.
Within them the slices are suspended:
pickling, orange fingers.

This is a beautiful place.

The store is hollow and the music,
it's also hollow. Someone should fix
the flashing fluorescent lights.

Colleen searches her purse
for breath mints. She sways.
She's still breathing.

I breathe with her. Then with the store.
Moments later I exhale with all of
Garrettsville, momentarily in-sync with

all the wild and trees and concrete and creek
and teachers and workers and other breathers
until the moment passes.

I place my tic tacs and salad ingredients
and frozen hamburgers on the counter.
I'm just a boy again.

Colleen Drinks to Think

and she blows in houses, the warm pre-storm.
High-stepping over toys, she learned to tip-toe
around black-eyed boys and hand-wringing girls.
She is challenged to ask *what* instead of *how* or *why*.

With Pastor John (who lets her call him just John)
the what of her spirits is in her spirit, drowning.
The spirit of Garrettsville, buried,
like a rusted time capsule. The spirit
of whiskey. The rusted whiskey spirits
of children, dancing like pinned butterflies.

Here whisky is a force of Nature
cheap power when washed down in waves
an artistic medium where
every canvas is soiled before
a drop of paint leaves the brush.

The rest of us know what Colleen knows,
but she has to catalogue the canoe oars,
broken and tossed in the creek. The bruises,
growing purpler still—Colleen's not allowed
to apply band aids.

After all, if she were to ever touch
the children
she'd be arrested.

5k in Ravenna

The food pantry is set up
across the blacktop. Volunteers
peddle shirts in a mess of tables.
The fire truck is leaking oil
which puddles under Judy.
She's a doughy woman baked
by the rugged independence of Ravenna.

A sullen, sleepless woman
points to a clipboard,
directs Alan, a bald man with knobs
for joints like the corded
branches of a tree. Nearby,
a boy pokes himself trying to attach 1206.

A runner stretches near a white
tent and coughs. Muriel's cigarette
smoke chokes him. The air is cold,
everyone is in sweats. The gun shot
will be less motivating today.

Runners are finishing the early race,
fruit flies stuck like black pepper
to their teeth. A girl tears
the race stub. Sweat and tears
commix over windburn.

The clouds: rolling cumulonimbus
ride like horses, ready to shake free
its cold gale and sweep us off the field—

like my mother rinsing
bits of vegetables from the bristling canyons
scored across the cutting board.

The Pastor's Gift

Pastor John gave me a key shaped like a rabbit. The rusted metal breathed in my hand, the puling precipice of sacrifice. We played Hot or Cold all the way to the Devil's Ice Box hidden behind a waterfall. A waterfall! A hissing body of water redirected from its source. Was it not always that way? I swept back the droplets, a shapely curtain that stained my clothes like ink. I couldn't find the lock, so I buried the chipped bunny in the swollen belly of sand and rocks. The ground trembled thank you, passing the Curse of Others to me with a slap on my shoulders that felt like Uncle Bob, but was more likely God. But I am no exhibitionist. No, not anymore. Now that I've buried the key I'm a waterfall, draining my innards into some ghastly garbage disposal, waiting by the curb. Sniffed at by rabbits. Waiting. Dug through by raccoons. Rotting, until I'm carted away.

Emma Performs My Baptism

Her hand brushes my forehead. I'm
not ready for the kiss against my ear.
Emma, she whispers my sins, lights
my cigarette, then chews my food for me.
What are men to rocks and mountains?

But when she leans in to whisper to me,
her lips are cracked. There's a patch in her hair
where she's scratched and scratched.
I don't demand answers, but Emma? I'm afraid
she'll remember me from yesterday.

Emma is a firecracker and bursts into flames.
I dipped my hand into a well, but I've
only found marrow. Faith saved the Jews
but anger drove them back to the desert.

As the water covers my forehead, Emma
performs a cross over my beating heart.
With the sun shining on me I dissolve.
Emma drops her contacts in the water
and puts the cigarette out on my eye.
God sees this and closes his gates
afraid Emma will get inside.

Gravel Laid Under Concrete

Every yesterday is a clipped sunflower
ripe for memory, overpriced.
A split pistil. Cloyed scrutiny.
Chalky happenings are smooth
fertilizers cascading down my arms,
perfect for growing more flowers.

The Body

Richard made his peace with God,
then crammed guilt into his suicide note
for the survivors. He fell twenty-two stories.

The first-floor tenants included young Jack
who watched for ten days. The chalk outline's
white dust seemingly melted away.

Family Practice

The dentist always ignores the words
etched into my jaw. But today my checkup
is with the doctor. Today I was plastic,
a chair in the lobby. The gum under my seat
is dirtier than me—I wash my hands.

In Room 207 I became a stool with a wrinkled cushion. The
faded composite cracks underneath, divots from fingernails
pressing
from white-knuckled patients.

Today Dr. Leu missed the rhythm in my heart.
I drive away from the office, and real life returns to focus.
I can again look for a five-leaf clover
and drink coffee from a mug.

One may find both hidden in the uncut grass.
These leaves of grass obscure skeletons.
My color comes back when I hit the brakes
for turkeys crossing the road.

And when I see a buzzard
ripping the intestines
from a squirrel smeared flat
my pulse finally returns.

Headwaters Trail

Cross country took me places. Every practice we
trailed down sidewalks snaking through town.
We saw our little sights: the football team practicing in their
field, the Pepsi guy taking his daily trek to Dairy Queen, and
elderly Mary Jane blowing off steam on her back porch.

Headwaters, a town staple surrounded by
birch, oak, and maple is an eight mile stretch of crushed
stone. Connected to Mantua,
it crosses a continental watershed divide
between the Mahoning and Cuyahoga River sheds.
Mahoning leads to the Gulf of Mexico,
the Cuyahoga up to the North Atlantic.

Native Americans named our county "Portage,"
or "to carry," because they carried canoes overhead between
these two watersheds.

Along this legacy we'd run several times a month and
complain about the workouts. Some walked the long
stretches where the tall grasses hid them. Others talked
during runs—independently confessional, collectively
priests.

Turkeys crossed the flat, sandy path in flocks,
black-feathered beggars laden with red bags.

Crickets hopped over mangled toads
and snakes, smeared under bike tracks.

Killdeer trill to protect their nest from predators
while song sparrows chirped in cadences
too specific for me to pick apart their meaning.

In this serenity the team sweat together, broke bread
together, and ultimately missed the Nature's lessons of
peace. At least until we'd grown, and,
learned how to look for it.

The Floral-Patterned Couch

My instincts were held hostage
upon the arrival of the white rabbit.

The rodent's ears bled,
shaken by your sacraments.

When I reoccupy this century
I'll call them lagomorphs.

Until then I'll recline, abated
memories sinking into melting snow.

Your rabbit ran unbound
nibbling at my carrots.

The couch was silent, hoisting
our sweaty frames, and—

I regret never kissing you back, but—
my instincts purred, correctly.

What it Means to Shed Skin

A tear falls upward
into my eyelid. Before long
I'm spitting oatmeal
back into my bowl.
I turn off the TV and lie down
as the sun sinks
back into the trees.
I lay down in a puddle of piss
and fall asleep wet.

> *I have a statuette of an elephant*
> *lifting water with her trunk.*
> *She is carved from marble,*
> *little toothpick tusks*
> *jutting into an imaginary*
> *lioness. I almost said no*
> *thank you at the gift shop*
> *on Main, but*
> *I'd recently lost my job.*

When I wake back up
I'm expecting a gunshot.
My paws thud the cracked earth
as I navigate the acacia forest.
When the elephant roars
I observe my new king.

Richard's Remains

After the accident, fresh asphalt was poured
over bits of crusted flesh.

The gods fought God
to tether Richard
to the manicured lawn
near his apartment.

Buried incomplete,
Richard wandered
without some minor memories.

He couldn't remember
his wife's middle name,
for example.

He forgot about his
ingrown toenail.

And now every time a deer
disturbs his ghastly routine
he's surprised to see it there.

Running Wild

A warren of paths spills outward
in the back ends of Bancroft
mostly through trees and fields—
scrambling green.

Samuel Brady dashed naked
through here just before his leap.

Sometimes floating above pine needle
and maple leaf beds I see Shawnee ghosts.
The more aware make faces at hunters,
but the rest weave rush mats
and wrestle in imaginary rings.

Local hunters often hear a baby
screeching from a pyre. This phantasm
is typically mistaken for wild turkeys.
Their rifles are slung sideways
across nylon and Velcro, carrot orange.

This forest trundles along.
Larch points along pools,
hazelnut billows, the white oak stretches,
a penetrating tribal beat. Hunting cats
stalk to this tune, lightning strikes
at this wavelength. The ocean
expands and recedes with similar
frequencies—the volatile yet familiar
power of Mother Nature

washing across humanity.

I cannot find the beat no matter
how I try. When I run after dark
I become acutely aware of vines
seemingly pulling the trees away from me
like hushed mothers guiding their children
from jabbering homeless.

Interstate 77 in '07

Everyone I meet nowadays
is a taxidermist, hungry,

walking the busiest highways
with a pick stick and spatula.

The White Birch Grove

A discarded mattress
suffocates in a bed of leaves
at the grove's center.

Each coil, a rusted tooth
soiled by mossy gingivitis.
The smile is dazzling.

I sleep, meditating on this stern
reminder of choice. The earthy
aromatics rise around me.

Twelve Years Later I Return Home

The kitchen is just a nook with a stove.
Dried water spots cluster in the corner,
dragging the paint with it. Inside the trash
is a pile of compost. I hope the dirt
was shoveled inside.

In the hall the grandfather clock is still
resonating. Is this the house's beating heart?
If so, where is the liver? The sinusoidal waves
drum through my ears, the only familiarity left
in this old, broken home.

The dining room is still painted "Patio Stone."
My parents were furious at how different
the swatch looked. I thought and think it is
nice. Yet the floors are still plywood,
soft after all those sunsets.

The living room ceiling fan is dusty.
A cobweb sags between the hanging
chains, and the self-portrait of
Raisin, a Dog, and a Vase With Arms
mounted on the wall, overseeing
claw marks in the hardwood, and,
maple branches clawing the front windows,
the window air conditioner teetering,
unsecured. How did that rusty metal frame
ever stay up?

The tree knocking on the window
waves
yawns
and
surrenders a very human shrug
before continuing its watch.

This tree is serene.
Someday the house will be, too.

The Recurring Dream

After I fell asleep soldiers
descended upon Bancroft.

I witnessed drunks, drafted,
fight the battle, only to drown

in their bathtubs. My aunt
took me in. She built

a blanket fort, lit candles,
and never came out again.

She didn't feed her daughter,
who starved in a dirty pile

of laundry. When I ran to find
help, my grandmother heard, but

misdialed 9-1-1. By the time
she could remember how

to dial correctly, a candle tipped
igniting her skirt. I cried so

my tears would fall into the ashes.
No phoenix emerged.

I wandered from room to room

wondering why the house was so big
and why my toys were all broken.

The Surgeon That Operates in the Dark

Emma tells me she has no
notion of loving people
by halves. With that,
she cuts me open with a rusted
scalpel in her unwashed hands.

Her incision is violent—
a shark's tooth dislodged
in the gasping flutter, folds
of bitter bone and tissue.

I'm peeled. My blood
creates antibodies against
Emma under a swinging,
lightless fixture. Her blouse
is stuffed into my open
chest cavity, reckless love.

A beau geste kiss upon
my exposed liver, Emma.
In silence still. Her eyes—
eroded stars, light years
before I learned they
had already burned out.

She stitches me up with
the care of a rabid beaver
gnawing logs, damming
my smoky tumors inside
with the blood-soaked blouse.

The Hero Hunt

I hunt to be a Disney Princess
draped in finches, chipmunks, moss.

Imagine the stone that held Excalibur:
living rock dressed in animal skins,
blood running into rivulets
joining riffles that sink
into a cavernous heart.

An archaeologist will note:
the dinosaurs died here
when the boy was just a mountain.
I kill here, atop the uppermost sediment
where this hill of a man
shrinks into a burial ground.

An engineer will one day build
a 7-Eleven on this plateau,
littered with bones.
A fossilized field
atop a brittle, cantankerous
old flint, patiently awaiting a hero.

The hunters will keep spoiling
meat, long after they need to hunt.
And Darwin will dance in his grave.

What I Pursue on Walks

Smoke curling above a matchstick, flung atop
a rotting stump slips into my senses. James is

out clearing Autumn's unattended leaf piles,
his pipe's cherry tobacco overpowering the cold

air. Further down, the smell of campfire smoke
contributes, penetrating layers of evergreen

suppressed by frost near the Workman's home, whose fence
is peeling its white paint like aging

zebra stripes. The pond is frozen—but if you listen carefully,
the frogs still ribbit

despite their hibernation. Vines slither up oak, curling
branches: dragons native to Ohio

with forked tongues, budded eyes, bearing witness to the
spirits of this gravel ribbon road.

Deep within the road's bare trunks, demons
and angels grapple over desecrated ground

behind the horse stables at the end of the street, where moss
grows on all sides of a tree trunk,

despite the folklore. Charlie's old blueberry fields are fallow,
waiting for a set of crusty

hands skilled in persuading the land
to give up its secrets. This area too, is frozen.

I can still smell the campfire a half mile away—
Mr. Workman is fanning the flames, and

cooking potatoes wrapped in foil, buried in gleaming coals.
A mile from home the spirits

rage in the open field at the end of the street. No deference is
demanded—no houses are here.

Just an empty field where I watched old man Jenson fly his
plane back when he mowed,

back when he was alive, back before the spirits took charge
of Bancroft.

Emma, Whom I Met in Death

I

Emma, I spread my hands, filthy
from your garden, across your mouth.
Your tongue licks larvae from my palms,
and I watch your throat hungrily
swallow them down.

Emma, just a couple of letters away,
Emma, just the postage—
you followed me on your bike
eight miles
then laid on my stomach.
Thrashing, Mother Nature
snoring in the next room,
my fingers down Emma's skirt.

Emma, chopping vegetables
irresistible, livery,
lively, I'd steal a soul for you
because you taught me how
to grow carrots and crush bone meal.
I'd do it again and again
until I missed my hands
like a ghosting amputee.

II

I filled the hollowed trunk
with gasoline and lit
the anthill massing inside.
Thousands of raving exoskeletons
sprang from the decaying torch.
Emma laughed, dumping a bucket of brine.

And Emma. There you are
in a library parking lot,
a pre-negotiated treaty.
The damnable hell of forged art.

I'm hurried now. Emma, my breathing—
irregular, I come, wishing the dishes
showed me your face when I cleaned them.
Laugh as much as you choose
but you will not laugh me out of my kitchen.

I forgot to clean this sink. Maggots grow
between the dirty utensils, pulsing.
Emma stands behind me, but between
the pulsing grub cascading against dishes
in a desperate attempt to usurp Nature's will
I only see my own face.

To come full-circle out of Garrettsville
I buried my various prejudices, combated
pride. I'll take the town with me wherever I go
as long as I'm still alive.

Acknowledgments

I would like to thank the following journals in which these poems, or earlier versions, originally appeared:

"Family Practice" *2018 Hessler Poetry Anthology*, May 2018

"What I Pursue on Walks" *Common Ground Review*, Summer 2018

"The White Birch Grove" *Right Hand Pointing*, Issue 120, March 2018

"The Garrettsville Boardwalk" CCPL Read & Write Spotlight, April 2018

"Richard's Remains" *West Side Poetry Workshop Anthology*, Spring 2018

"The Body" *West Side Poetry Workshop Anthology*, Spring 2018

"Fluid Motion" *Eunoia Review*, Jan 2018

"Headwaters Trail" *Cartwright Lit Poetry*, March 2016

"The Garrettsville Boardwalk" *2015 Hessler Poetry Anthology*, May 2015

"Parking Lot Paint" *Eunoia Review*, May 2015

"Family Practice" *Right Hand Pointing*, Issue 85, April 2015

"4 AM" *Songs of Eretz Poetry Review,* Dec 2014

"State Route 422" *Songs of Eretz Poetry Review,* Dec 2014

"Nelson Ledges State Park" *The Rusty Nail,* Issue 20, Sept/Oct 2014

"Brad's Liquor Stop" *The Rusty Nail,* Issue 20, Sept/Oct 2014

"Breakfast" *Maple Axle,* 2013

About the Author

Jeremy Jusek is a poet and writer living in Cleveland, Ohio with his wife and two kids. He left Marietta College with degrees in chemistry and theatre and went on to earn his MFA in Creative Writing from the Arcadia University.

When he's not writing or daddying, Jeremy spends his free time running, gardening, playing video games, and nursing coffee ulcers.

For more information on his background and publications please visit www.jeremyjusek.com.

About the Press

Unsolicited Press was founded in 2012 and is located in Portland, Oregon. The team worked to produce outstanding poetry, fiction, and creative nonfiction. Learn more at www.unsolicitedpress.com.

www.ingramcontent.com/pod-product-compliance
Lightning Source LLC
Chambersburg PA
CBHW020130130526
44591CB00032B/581